Get Out Of Debt: In A Few Easy Steps (Credit Card, Mortgages)

Complete Information on How to Regain your Credit Score

By: Amy Reed

9781634289788

PUBLISHERS NOTES

Disclaimer – Speedy Publishing LLC

This book was originally printed before 2014. This is an adapted reprint by Speedy Publishing LLC with newly updated content designed to help readers with much more accurate and timely information and data.

Speedy Publishing LLC

40 E Main Street, Newark, Delaware, 19711

Contact Us: 1-888-248-4521

Website: http://www.speedypublishing.co

REPRINTED Paperback Edition: ISBN: 9781634289788

Manufactured in the United States of America

DEDICATION

I dedicate this book to my mother, Amelia. I give all the credits to her. She was able to raise me well and always a loving and supportive mother to me.

TABLE OF CONTENTS

Chapter 1- An Overview on What Debt and Credit Report Means

We are a country in debt. Not only is our government in debt, but we, as Americans, are in debt ourselves, and the problem is just getting worse! Recent studies have shown that ninety percent of Americans have at least one credit card – and they are using that card – A LOT!

The average family carries a balance of between $7,000 and $10,000 on all their credit cards. Over $1,000 per family goes on interest every year. And that's just the average – some people owe much more!

Overall, Americans spend over $1 trillion every year on their credit cards, and owe more than $500 billion of it. If debt continues at the current rate, then one family in a hundred will be forced into bankruptcy. Over 90% of Americans' disposable incomes are spent paying back debts.

Get Out of Debt

When you add credit card debt to the regular bills we have to pay each month, which can tax anyone's budget. As a result, some bills go unpaid and others are paid late.

Both of these instances can damage your credit sometimes so much that you think there's no way you'll ever be able to get out of debt and get credit for something important like a home or a car.

The truth is that you can get out of debt and repair your credit nearly to what it was before you had credit problems. It takes some time and a little work on your part, but it IS possible.

Loan approvals and such depend on your credit score. That number is what determines if you can get credit, what your interest rate will be, and how much money potential lenders will give you. A good median score is 750, but the higher your score is, the more financially sound you are.

While it's always a good idea to try and stay away from credit, not everyone has a hundred thousand dollars lying around to buy a home or twenty thousand to buy a car. Heck, for some people, scraping together five thousand dollars for a good used car is difficult. That's why we need credit. So we can buy that which we cannot afford.

Where the trouble comes in is when people begin to buy everyday items such as groceries and clothing on credit cards. Then those bills begin to get bigger and bigger until pretty soon, they're paying the minimum amount due which will take forever to pay off. Plus, a lot of people just continue charging things even when they have a large balance on their account.

Your credit score defines who you are to businesses and you want it to be as high as it can be. It doesn't matter how bad your credit is now. There are ways that you can raise your credit score no matter how low it is now. Don't despair; just get started – right away!

CHAPTER 2- HISTORY OF FICO – FAIR ISAAC

Back in the 1960's, a company called Fair Isaac devised a unique system to determine the credit worthiness of people who apply for loans. Through a complicated mathematical computation, they were able to study a person's credit history and assign them a number that would represent how likely it was that they would be able to repay a loan they were applying for.

Fair Isaac sparked a revolution by pioneering credit risk scoring for the financial services industry. This new approach to lending enabled financial institutions to improve their business performance and expand consumers' access to credit.

Today Fair Isaac's FICO score is widely recognized as the industry standard for lenders.

The FICO score condenses a borrower's credit history into a single number based on past credit history. Fair, Isaac & Co. and the credit bureaus do not reveal how these scores are computed. The

Federal Trade Commission has ruled this to be acceptable. The real truth is that even if we did know, we probably couldn't calculate it ourselves anyway. Unless, of course, you happen to be a mathematical genius!

Credit scores are calculated by using scoring models and mathematical tables that assign points for different pieces of information which best predict future credit performance. Developing these models involves studying how thousands, even millions, of people have used credit.

Score-model developers find predictive factors in the data that have proven to indicate future credit performance. Models can be developed from different sources of data. Credit-bureau models are developed from information in consumer credit-bureau reports.

Credit scores analyze a borrower's credit history considering numerous factors such as:

• Late payments

• The amount of time credit has been established

• The amount of credit used versus the amount of credit available

• Length of time at present residence

• Negative credit information such as bankruptcies, charge-offs, collections, etc.

There are really three FICO scores computed by data provided by each of the three bureaus—Experian, Trans Union and Equifax.

Get Out of Debt

Some lenders use one of these three scores, while other lenders may just use the middle score.

Fair Isaac has become so important in the financial industry that their word on your credit has become basically the final word. Why would banks and creditors place so much credibility into one company? The answer is simply because of their proven track record.

The FICO score has proven to be not only an accurate and amazingly consistent way of showing a person's credit reliability, but it has also saved companies millions of dollars in credit write-offs due to bad lending decisions. A study of loans that were granted and/or denied simply due to the FICO scores shows that Fair Isaac has been right over 80 percent of the time.

Of course, that required some chance taking on the part of many creditors, but they were willing to take the risk. After all, this was a ground-breaking thing determining credit worthiness through a simple three-digit number. Many companies jumped "on the bandwagon" just to show that Fair Isaac had the right idea.

Fast forward to the twenty-first century and you will find that FICO has become the definitive when it comes to financial and credit matters. They have proven their reliability and their worthiness just through trial and error.

Unfortunately, the problem is that finding your FICO score isn't as easy as you think. The truth is that it's not even shown on your credit report like you would think. In fact, for years and years, your credit score was a securely kept secret number that was elusive to the average person.

How to Find your FICO

You would think that finding out what your credit score is would be easy. In a way it is, but only because I've done my research and you won't have to spend time surfing websites looking for the ever elusive credit number. It would seem logical to have your credit score appear right on your credit report, but that's just not the way it is.

At one time, your credit score was a big secret known only to financial companies and banks. With the FACT Act, legislators decided that it was important for individuals to know not only what their personal credit scores are but how they are calculated and how to improve them.

The main company who calculates your credit score is the Field, Isaac Company commonly known as FICO. They invented the concept of the FICO scores so they are the ones who are known as experts in the industry. Before we go into finding your score, let's look at a few facts about the FICO score.

- FICO scores are your credit rating
- They range from 300-850, higher is better
- Most lenders base approval on them
- Higher scores mean lower interest rates
- FICO scores are calculated based on your rating in five general categories:
    - Payment history - 35%
    - Amounts owed - 30%
    - Length of credit history - 15%
    - New credit - 10%
    - Types of credit used - 10%

- Field, Isaac Company is the inventor of the FICO score
- They have the only website offering all 3 of your FICO scores
- The median FICO score in the U.S. is 723

Essentially, your credit score is simply a snapshot of your credit use - it's the Cliffs Notes version of seven years of your borrowing history. In many lending situations, the lender bases its decision almost solely on your credit score.

Consider your credit score the overall GPA of your borrowing history.

Now, here's the bad news. If you want to know your actual credit score, you will usually have to purchase it. This can be done in a few ways.

You can get it from one of the three major credit reporting companies: Equifax, Experian, and TransUnion. The fee isn't a huge one – usually around $15 or $20.

However, if you're serious about growing your credit score, it's well worth the money to be financially responsible in the end.

They will offer you a free 30 day trial membership which will get your credit score right now and then, if you wish to continue the membership, it will update the score as it rises (or, heaven forbid lowers).

If you are applying for a mortgage, here's a little good news for you. You can find out your credit score for free! The mortgage company will base their decision and interest rate on what your credit score number is, so just ask and they'll tell you!

FICO scores range between 300 and 850. Here's what those scores mean:

- Over 750 – you have excellent credit and will be able obtain credit easily
- 720 or more – you still have very good credit and will be able to obtain credit easily
- 660 to 720 – this is an acceptable credit. You can still get loans, but you may pay a higher interest rate
- 620 to 660 – creditors are going to be uncertain about lending you money
- Less than 620 – you have poor credit history and will probably not be able to obtain credit on your own.

Knowing the above information makes it obvious that if you need or want to get credit for something, the higher your score is, the better your chances are to not only get credit but get it at a handsome interest rate. If you are in the 660 to 620 range, you may still get a loan, but the interest rate is likely to be higher.

That's why it's important to keep your credit good or establish good credit from the get go. That's where we'll start.

How Credit Cards Work

If you want to eliminate your credit card debt you have to understand what credit is.

In case you haven't figured it out yet, the credit system works against you, unless you are prepared.

And since it is an unfair game, you need to know the rules. Once you know how credit works, how compound interest works, you can start using it to your advantage, instead of being a victim of it.

Get Out of Debt
Here are some facts you need to know.

In 2005, a record 6 billion "pre-approved" credit card offers were mailed to consumers. By comparison, only 10 years before, in 1995, 2.7 billion offers were mailed out.

These offers usually carry a "low introductory" rate which is "fixed" for a set number of months. But, once you read the fine print, you find out that in reality that "fixed" rate can change at any time, and for any reason. What follows was taken from an offer I recently received from Chase Bank.

"Rates, Fees and terms may change: We reserve the right to change the terms of your account (including the APRs) at any time, for any reason, in addition to APR increases that may occur for failure to comply with the terms of your account" (underlying is mine)

So you may be thinking you are getting a great deal, when in reality they can change the rules whenever they want.

Unfortunately, you cannot beat the system. They write the rules to their advantage and we must comply. Every year, credit card companies, banks and financial institutions spend millions and millions of dollars lobbying Congress to make sure laws are passed that benefit them, not consumers.

You simply cannot compete.

The good news is that you don't need to beat the system; you just need to understand it.

Pre-approved offers are mailed to anyone on a list that a credit card company purchases (usually from the Credit Bureaus), and does not mean that you will definitely get a credit card. They are inviting you to apply, but they are targeting their mailings towards consumers who are more likely to respond and qualify for a card.

If you do not want to receive any more offers, you can call (888)567-8688 to request that Credit Bureaus not include your file in any pre-approved / promotional lists. I encourage you to opt-out, if (for no other reason) to minimize the chances of identity theft.

If you prefer to contact the Bureaus directly, write to the following addresses and tell them you want to opt-out of pre-approval screening:

Equifax Options:

P O Box 7401243 - Atlanta, GA 30374-0123 (800)556-4711

Experian Consumer Opt Out

701 Experian Parkway - Allen, TX 75013 (800)353-0809

TransUnion

Attn: Marketing Opt Out   PO Box 97328 – Jackson, MS 39288-7328

(800) 680-7293

There are several more practices that have become more common in the last few years.

One of them is the "Grace Period", which is the number of days you have to repay your purchase before you are charged interest.

Get Out of Debt

Many cards have reduced the grace period from 30 days down to 21 days. With a 21-day grace period you have less time to pay for your purchases in full, and a better chance of paying interest than before. And, if the amount is not paid in full, interest is charged from the date of purchase, not the day you started financing it.

Another practice is the addition of the over-the-limit fee. Many consumers would expect their credit card to be declined if a transaction would put the card over their credit limit. But, increasingly, credit card companies are allowing these transactions to go through, and then slapping consumers with an over-the-limit fee of $20, $25 or more.

Late fees are escalating too, adding $30 to $50 to your credit card bill. Not to mention that your interest rate skyrockets. I personally know someone in New York who sent his payment in late, and his interest rate went from 9% to 29% the following month. This is very common.

There is also the Foreign Transaction fee that you get hit with when withdrawing your money from an ATM outside of the States. Keep that in mind next time you travel.

Simply withdrawing money from an ATM that doesn't belong to the bank means you are going to be hit with two fees. One fee that is charged by the bank that owns the ATM and another fee that is charged by your bank (not all banks will charge this fee, but most will). Withdrawing $20 from another bank's ATM could result in $4 to $6 in fees. How many times a year do you withdraw money from other bank's ATMs?

There are way too many fees to list here, but you get the idea.

Are you asking yourself what you can do to protect yourself?

There are a number of things you can do.

First, you need to check your credit card statements every month. Believe it or not, most people do not check their statements. Check not only your credit card statements but also your checking account and your savings account statements. Look for any errors.

Look for fees, and see if they are correct. If you see any over-the-limit or late fees, call the company and ask (politely) if they can waive them. They will usually waive them, but if you are late again or over the limit again, they may not do it a second time.

Be very careful when mailing your payments. Send them at least 10 days before the due date to avoid late fees. Or set it up so the balance is deducted from your checking or savings account automatically. Contact your bank to find out how to do it.

You can also (and I encourage you to do this) call your credit card companies and ask for a reduction of your interest rate. This may be a little harder to get, but if they don't want to do it, don't despair. Call again in a couple of weeks, and ask again. In Part 2 you can read a script you can use when you call.

What is compound interest?

This is the most important concept to understand if you plan to stay debt free forever.

And for you to understand exactly how it works, I'll ask you a question: What would you rather have, a million dollars in cash right now, or one penny today, two pennies tomorrow, four pennies the next day, eight pennies the next one and so on for the next 30 days?

Get Out of Debt

Most people would choose the million dollars, and it is a good choice, I mean, who wouldn't want a million dollars? However, the second option is much better. Look at the following table to see the power of compound interest in action:

Day 1: $.01

Day 2: $.02

Day 3: $.04

Day 4: $.08

Day 5: $.16

Day 6: $.32

Day 7: $.64

Day 8: $1.28

Day 9: $2.56

Day 10: $5.12

Day 11: $10.24

Day 12: $20.48

Day 13: $40.96

Day 14: $81.92

Day 15: $163.84

Day 16: $327.68

Day 17: $655.36

Day 18: $1,310.72

Day 19: $2,621.44

Day 20: $5,242.88

Day 21: $10,485.76

Day 22: $20,971.52

Day 23: $41,943.04

Day 24: $83,386.08

Day 25: $167,772.16

Day 26: $335,544.32

Day 27: $671,088.64

Day 28: $1,342,177.28

Day 29: $2,684,354.56

Day 30: $5,368,709.12

This is the magic of compound interest. A penny doubled every day may not seem like much, but the compounding factor is incredible. In fact, Albert Einstein has been quoted as saying "The most powerful force in the universe is compound interest."

Get Out of Debt

As you can see in the table above, a penny doubled every day gives you over $5,000,000 in just 30 days. This is how powerful compound interest is. And this is what credit card companies are using against you.

When you make charges on your credit card, you pay interest on any balance you carry (balance would be any unpaid amount on your credit card statement). This interest is calculated not only on the initial principal but also the accumulated interest of prior periods.

Compound interest can really hurt you, especially if you are making the minimum payment on each of your credit cards. When you carry a balance, compound interest is calculated daily, which means every day interest is added to your balance. If you pay the minimum payment on a credit card, you are only making the bank richer.

To show you compound interest in action, consider that if you have a credit card with $5,000 balance at 18% a year, and you were to pay only the minimum payment (let's say it's 3% of your balance), it would take you 199 months to pay it off! (Assuming that the rate doesn't change and you never use your card again). So your account will be paid off in exactly 199 months (over 16 years!) and you will have paid $4,698.46 in interest. This is insane. This is what banks don't want you to know. Send them only the minimum payment and they will love you forever.

How home mortgage loans work

If you own your own home you may not even think of your mortgage as debt. You may even believe that the house is really yours. You need to understand how mortgage loans work if you want to be truly debt-free.

Page | 20

Home mortgages operate the same way that credit cards do. The difference is that mortgage companies will never say that the interest on their loans is compounded daily (maybe on their fine print, buried among hundreds of pages that you sign at closing). But now that you understand how compound interest works, you may start to realize that it only makes sense to pay off your mortgage as soon as possible.

Most people just assume that the interest on their mortgage is simple interest. When they get a 6% interest rate, they think that the interest they pay will be 6% of the total amount they financed, calculated yearly. This is what I found out after talking to my clients. But nothing could be further from the truth. In reality, if you paid off your whole mortgage in one year, then yes, the interest rate would be 6% (well, actually a little more because of the compounding effect, but I'm trying to illustrate a point here). But if it is paid over 30 years, then the actual interest rate is well over 100%! Think about it! You could buy more than 2 houses with the same money!

The reason that the interest rate is so important is that you're paying compound interest, not simple interest. The higher the interest rate, then obviously, the more interest you will pay. I have seen people with a 9.8% interest on their $300,000 loan; in 30 years they will have paid over $631,000 in interest alone! That's over 200% interest!

These examples are worrisome; however, they do not compare to the other types of mortgage loans that are causing so many people lose their homes.

One of them is the so called "Interest Only" loans. Basically you only pay the interest portion of the payment, deferring the difference (thereby accumulating interest, which is added to your account). It means that you are not only NOT paying down the balance of your loan, but you are also adding more interest (you are adding interest to the balance you didn't yet pay). If property values are going up, then it may not be a bad loan in some specific cases (i.e., buying a house with the intention of selling it in a few months); however, in a declining market it is financial suicide. The only way somebody would benefit from an Interest Only mortgage loan is if they were sending some money to be applied towards the principal every month and the interest rate is substantially lower than they had before (if they are refinancing). On purchases it was a good option when houses were appreciating very fast, as was the case in many parts of the country not too long ago, but obviously very risky. In today's market, it's definitely not an option to consider.

The riskiest mortgage loans available are called Option ARM (Adjustable Rate Mortgage) or Pick a Pay loans. Every month, you get to pick which payment (out of four) you will send to the mortgage company. This is a good option for professionals or business owners whose income fluctuates sharply from month to month, but definitely NOT for most people.

With option 1 you send less than that month's interest (which means, the difference is added to the balance, collecting more interest.) For example, let's take a $200,000 loan with a Fully Amortizing rate (the real rate that would pay off the loan in 30 years) of 7.683% and a minimum payment rate of 1.25%. The option one payment will be $666.50 (deferring $614 of the interest that was due that month, which automatically is added to the balance and starts collecting interest)

With option 2, you send only the interest for that month (which means, you are not paying down the balance, or explained differently, it's as if you were like "renting" the house! Following the previous example, you would send $1,280.60 for that month, but the balance is not paid down.

With option 3, you send the regular payment (principal and interest) calculated over 30 years. In this example, it will be $1,423.58.

And with option 4 you send the regular payment calculated over 15 years instead of 30, but it will be obviously substantially higher. Following our example that payment would be $1,874.88

Can you guess which payment most people usually send?

I have seen mortgage statements from banks where the option that is highlighted in the payment coupon (or in big, bold letters) is always the minimum payment (option 1). This leads people to believe that's the payment they should send, and many people send just that. One of my clients added $60,000 to his mortgage loan in just 2 ½ years without realizing what was going on. In my experience, many people were not well informed when they were offered these loans.

Option Arm loans can spell trouble, especially when property values decline and home owners owe more than their house is worth. To add insult to injury, when people refinance they discover that the interest rate is always higher on an Option Arm loan than on a 30-year fixed loan! Fortunately, these types of loans are not as popular in the US right now as they were in the early 2000's.

As you can see, ignorance is not bliss, is expensive.

Many people believe that paying off their mortgage is a bad financial decision, and they have two arguments to back up this position. I respect both arguments, but I do not agree with either one. The first argument is that a home mortgage has tax benefits (since mortgage interest can be deducted from your taxes); the second is that since the interest on a mortgage is usually low (around 4 to 6% in the last few years depending on many factors like your credit, etc), you will benefit by making regular payments to your mortgage lender and investing your discretionary income elsewhere, as long as the interest on your investment is higher than the interest on your mortgage.

Let's look at both arguments. As far as the mortgage interest being tax deductible, what it really means is that if you pay, let's say, $10,000 in mortgage interest in a given year, you will save $2,500 in taxes (if you are at a 25% bracket; it would be even less money if you are at a lower bracket!). Think about this for a moment. Does it really make financial sense to you? Paying the bank $10,000 to get back $2,500? If you are like me, it will not make any sense at all. It makes more sense to pay off the mortgage, and once it's paid off, you get to KEEP the $10,000 (or whatever you would have paid in interest) as disposable income or as investment money.

As far as investing your money somewhere else that could give you a higher return (higher than your mortgage interest), let me offer the following facts to you: whatever interest you pay on your mortgage, will be the GUARANTEED interest you will make by paying it off (or paying it down). You cannot guarantee the performance of any other investment, as you probably already know. Market conditions fluctuate and could affect your investments; however, paying off your 6% mortgage is a guaranteed 6 % "return".

And let's face it, most people, including myself, are not keen investors. Many will have a Mutual Fund or retirement account that they rarely review, and investing does take a lot of planning and research. Without proper planning and research you could be "throwing darts" at your financial future, when you consider this, then paying off your mortgage early does make financial sense due to its simplicity and high return. However, if you are a keen investor, then it may make sense not to pay off your mortgage and invest your discretionary income somewhere else.

In the next part, I will show you a way to pay off ALL your debt, including your mortgage, in record time. This method is not about refinancing your home, it is not about debt consolidation, nor is it about debt settlement. It is based on a surprisingly simple (and incredibly powerful) formula that will give you the financial freedom you and your family deserve. This system will work even if you are under a debt consolidation program or if you have student loans.

Chapter 3- Establishing, Building and Maintaining Good Credit Score

So you don't have any credit to speak of, but you have big plans for the future.

Maybe you're a fresh college graduate or a young person eager to buy your first new car.

If you have never had to use credit before, first of all BRAVO! Of course, it's best to pay cash for the things you need so that you don't have to worry about credit card payments, loan payments, or interest rates.

But if you're young, the chances of you needing credit in the future are very real. Someday you might want to buy a house. Perhaps you'll want to buy a new car.

Chances are pretty good that you won't have the cash outright to buy these high ticket items which mean you'll need credit. Plus, it's always good to have a little credit since many utility companies will look at your credit to turn on your power bill, for example, without a deposit of some type.

When you're starting fresh with no credit history at all, here are a few ways to get a good start on establishing good credit:

1. Pay your bills on time, especially mortgage or rent payments. Apart from extreme circumstances like bankruptcy or tax liens, nothing has as big of an impact on your credit history as late payments.

2. Establish credit early. Having clean, active charge accounts established many years ago will boost your score. If you are averse to credit, on principle, consider setting up automatic monthly payments for, say, utilities and phone on a credit card account and locking the card away where it's not a temptation.

3. Don't max out available credit on credit card accounts. Lenders won't be impressed. Instead, they are much more likely to assume that you have trouble managing your finances. Beyond one or two credit cards, it starts to get complicated.

4. Don't apply for too much credit in a short amount of time. Multiple requests for your credit history (not including requests by you to check your file) will reduce your score. If you are hunting around for good loan rates, assume that every time you give your

Social Security number to a lender or credit card company, they will order a credit history.

5. Be neat and consistent when filling out credit applications. This will insure that all your good deeds get recorded in a single file, as opposed to multiple files or, worse, someone else's file. Watch out for inconsistencies in use of "Jr." and "Sr."

6. Check your credit history for errors, especially if you will soon be requesting a time-dependent loan, like a mortgage.

One great way to start establishing credit is to apply for a store credit card (Sears, JC Penney, etc.). Once you get the card, make a few small purchases and pay them off completely. Do this a few times over the course of a year and you'll find yourself with some established credit with an excellent payment history. DO NOT go overboard and buy more than what you can pay for, though.

You can also apply for a secured credit card. These cards ask that you place a certain amount of money in your account for which you will receive a charge card.

Then you can make purchases up to the amount of money that is in your account.

Credit reporting agencies treat these cards just like regular credit cards and look to them as a responsible way for you to establish a good credit history.

You will have to have a checking account to establish credit. This lends to your credibility with lenders and shows that you are able to manage your money effectively.

Amy Reed

When applying for a credit card of any type, be sure to ask if they report to any of the credit reporting agencies. As we've said before, they are not required to do so, and if they don't, having one of these cards or loans won't do you a lick of good even if you do make your payments on time.

You can also establish credit by making a purchase or applying for a loan with a co-signer. A co-signer is a person with good credit history who is basically telling the lending company that they will be responsible for making sure you make your payments on time. Often a co-signer is a relative such as a parent. This can be a risky proposition for them, so know that they are putting their own credit history on the line just to help you out, so don't let them down.

When applying for a loan, such as a car loan, it can also be helpful if you have a large down payment to make thus lessening the amount of money you have to borrow. This shows the lending company that you have the ability to save and they are more likely to take a chance on you based on this factor alone. So let's do a quick review on how to establish a good credit history:

- Apply for a store or gas credit card and make a few charges
- Ask a loved one to co-sign on a loan
- Find a respected secured credit card company
- Open a checking account
- Don't apply for too many credit cards in too short of a time
- Check your credit report for any errors
- Go slowly
- Don't overspend
- Make sure your lender reports to at least one of the credit reporting agencies
- MAKE YOUR PAYMENTS ON TIME!!!!!!!

Get Out of Debt

Of course, the last one is the most important in establishing credit. If you don't make your payments on time, it won't make a hill of beans worth of difference what you are trying to do. This is what makes your credit history worthwhile – making on time payments and showing you are responsible with your credit and your creditors.

So, what if you've already had credit, but you've made some mistakes over the years finding yourself with bad credit? Is all hope lost? The good news is – NO!

CHAPTER 4- HOW TO GET OUT OF DEBT - BANKRUPTCY

Filing for bankruptcy has a very negative connotation in society, but it's a way for people who have found themselves in serious financial trouble to ease the burden of what they've done and allow them to start over. Businesses don't like it, but for consumers, it can be a life saver.

This writer knows of one young girl – just 21 years old – who was over $20,000 in debt plus she had her car repossessed for non-payment. At this young age, she was in serious financial trouble with no way out.

She was (still is) going to school trying to earn a degree so she can get a good job, but since her first credit card was issued to her at age 17, her credit woes began and they didn't end until she was able to file for bankruptcy.

Her debts were discharged and she was able to start all over again. She purchased a (very) used vehicle for cash, got a part-time job while she went to school and worked very hard to build her credit up slowly.

Now she is 30. She has a well-paying job as a nurse at a local hospital and just celebrated buying her first home. She once told me, "I knew I was in over my head and I became very depressed because of it. The bankruptcy was the best thing I could have ever done for myself even though at the time, it was the hardest."

Let's start by exploring the different types of bankruptcies. Chapter 7, Chapter 11, and Chapter 13.

Chapter 7 bankruptcy, sometimes call a straight bankruptcy is a liquidation proceeding. The debtor turns over all non-exempt property to the bankruptcy trustee who then converts it to cash for distribution to the creditors.

The debtor receives a discharge of all dischargeable debts usually within four months. In the vast majority of cases the debtor has no assets that he would lose so Chapter 7 will give that person a relatively quick "fresh start".

One of the main purposes of Bankruptcy Law is to give a person, who is hopelessly burdened with debt, a fresh start by wiping out his or her debts.

New legislation has been passed regarding Chapter 7 bankruptcies. Laws can vary from state to state, so you will want to check with someone who knows or do extensive research as to what is allowed to be discharged with a Chapter 7 and what is not.

Essentially what the new laws ask of people who are filing a Chapter 7 bankruptcy is twofold. First, they must take an approved credit counseling course within six months before filing. They must also complete an approved financial management course before any debts can be discharged.

Even though those two new stipulations are in place, it is still relatively easy to file for a Chapter 7 bankruptcy. There are, of course, governmental "hoops" you will have to jump through which is why it is often a good idea to secure the services of a bankruptcy lawyer. However, it is possible for you to do this yourself as long as you do your research and "cross your T's and dot your I's"!

What are the most common reasons given for filing a Chapter 7 bankruptcy?

Well, of course, it's the accumulation of excessive debt! But seriously, here are the most common reasons why people get into such debt:

• Medical bills

• Unemployment

• Divorce

• Overextended credit

• Large, unexpected expense

A Harvard Study reported that half of US bankruptcies were caused by medical bills. The study was published online in February of 2005 by Health Affairs. The Harvard study concluded that illness and medical bills caused half (50.4 percent) of the 1,458,000 personal bankruptcies in 2001. The study estimates that medical bankruptcies affect about 2 million Americans annually — counting debtors and their dependents, including about 700,000 children.

If you find that you have to file for a Chapter 7 bankruptcy, you may be worried about whether or not you'll get to keep some of the things that are important to you and essential to life. These things include a car and your home, among other things.

Unsecured debts, such as credit card debt, personal loans, money judgments and certain taxes are wiped out in a Chapter 7. However, certain debts are not dischargeable under Chapter 7 bankruptcy; these debts include, but are not limited to, most student loans, certain taxes, alimony and child or other court ordered support payments.

If a debt is secured by property, such as a home mortgage or an automobile loan, then you get to decide how to handle that debt. For example, in the case of a vehicle, you could:

1. Keep the automobile and the debt as long as you are current and continue keeps your payments current.

2. "Redeem" the automobile which means pay it off at its current "fair market value"

3. Return the vehicle, include any balance due in your bankruptcy and pay nothing further on the vehicle. The choice is yours.

In 99% of the Chapter 7 cases, the person filing bankruptcy keeps all of their property. Bankruptcy law is not meant to punish you and allows you to keep your property under what are called "exemptions" or things you get to keep. You keep your car, your house, your jewelry, the boat, your clothing, everything!

Of course, if you still owe a debt on anything like your car and your house, you should refer to the above scenario. If you want to discharge your car loan, you'll have to either pay up or give up the car.

What is Chapter 13?

Another option for bankruptcy for individuals is the Chapter 13. This is more commonly known as a reorganization bankruptcy. Chapter13 bankruptcy is filed by individuals who want to pay off their debts over a period of three to five years.

This type of bankruptcy appeals to individuals who have non-exempt property that they want to keep. It is also only an option for individuals who have predictable income and whose income is sufficient to pay their reasonable expenses with some amount left over to pay off their debts.

There are many reasons why people choose Chapter 13 bankruptcy instead of Chapter 7 bankruptcy. Generally, you are probably a good candidate for Chapter 13 bankruptcy if you are in any of the following situations:

1. You have a sincere desire to repay your debts, but you need the protection of the bankruptcy court to do so. You may think filing Chapter 13 bankruptcy is simply the "Right Thing To Do" rather than file Chapter

2. You are behind on your mortgage or car loan, and want to make up the missed payments over time and reinstate the original agreement. You cannot do this in Chapter 7 bankruptcy. You can make up missed payments only in Chapter 13 bankruptcy.

3. You need help repaying your debts now, but need to leave open the option of filing for Chapter 7 bankruptcy in the future. This would be the case if for some reason you can't stop incurring new debt.

4. You are a family farmer who wants to pay off your debts, but you do not qualify for a Chapter 12 family farming bankruptcy because you have a large debt unrelated to farming.

5. You have valuable nonexempt property. When you file for Chapter 7 bankruptcy, you get to keep certain property, called exempt. If you have a lot of nonexempt property (which you'd have to give up if you file a Chapter 7 bankruptcy), Chapter 13 bankruptcy may be the better option.

6. You received a Chapter 7 discharge within the previous eight years. You cannot file for Chapter 7 again until the eight years are up.

A Chapter 13 can be filed if:

•The debtor received a discharge under Chapter 7, 11 or 12 more than four years ago

•The debtor received a discharge under Chapter 13 more than two years ago. You have a co-debtor on a personal debt. If you file for Chapter 7 bankruptcy, your creditor will go after the co-debtor for payment. If you file for Chapter 13 bankruptcy, the creditor will leave your co-debtor alone, as long as you keep up with your bankruptcy plan payments.

•You have a tax debt. If a large part of your debt consists of federal taxes, what happens to your tax debts may determine which type of bankruptcy is best for you.

As of October 17, 2005, new bankruptcy laws took effect for all three types of bankruptcy. When it comes to Chapter 13, you cannot file this way unless the following conditions are met:

•The debtor received a discharge under Chapter 7, 11 or 12 more than four years ago.

•The debtor received a discharge under Chapter 13 more than two years ago.

•When a motor vehicle was purchased within 910 days (2 1/2 years) of the filing and a secured creditor has a lien on it, the creditor retains the lien until payment of the entire debt has been made.

•The following debt is NOT discharged:

•debt for trust fund taxes;

•taxes for which returns were never filed or filed late (within two years of the petition date);

•taxes for which the debtor made a fraudulent return or evaded taxes;

•domestic support payments;

•Student loans;

•Drunk driving injuries;

•Criminal restitution;

Get Out of Debt

•Civil restitutions or damages awarded for willful or malicious personal actions causing personal injury or death.

• All tax returns for the four years prior to filing Chapter 13 must be filed.

•Debtors must provide to the trustee, at least seven days prior to the 341 meeting, a copy of a tax return or transcript of a tax return, for the period for which the return was most recently due.

What is Chapter 11

A Chapter 11 bankruptcy is filed by businesses and is quite similar to a Chapter 13. A Chapter 11 is available for individuals, but it is generally used by businesses to reorganize their debts and dealings so that they can be more financially solid.

When a troubled business is unable to service its debt or pay its creditors, they can file with a federal bankruptcy court for protection under either a Chapter 7 or a Chapter 11 bankruptcy.

In a Chapter 7 bankruptcy, the business must cease operation and a trustee will sell all its assets and distribute the proceeds to the business's creditors ratably in accordance with statutory priorities.

A Chapter 11 filing, on the other hand, is usually filed in an attempt to stay in business while a bankruptcy court supervises the reorganization of the company's contractual and debt obligations. The court can grant complete or partial relief from most of the company's debts along with its contracts so that the company can make a fresh start.

Often, if the company's debts exceed its assets, then at the completion of the bankruptcy, the company's owners or stockholders all end up with nothing. All their rights and interests are terminated and the company's creditors end up with ownership of the newly reorganized company in the hopes that it will eventually succeed financially as compensation for their losses.

So, in general, an individual bankruptcy will be under a Chapter 7 or Chapter 11.

It's a big decision for you to make, but sometimes, it's the only way you can "get out from under" and begin anew.

Before you resort to filing for a Chapter 7 or Chapter 11, consider the alternatives.

Creditors might be willing to settle their claim for a smaller cash payment, or they might be willing to stretch out the loan and reduce the size of the payments. This would allow you to pay off the debt by making smaller payments over a longer period of time. The creditor would eventually receive the full economic benefit of its bargain.

Occasionally, you may "buy time" by consolidating your debts; that is, by taking out a big loan to pay off all the smaller amounts of debts that you owe. The primary danger of this approach is that it is very easy to go out and use your credit cards to borrow even more.

In that case, you end up with an even larger total debt and no more income to meet the monthly payments. Indeed, if you have taken out a second mortgage on your home to obtain the consolidation loan, you might lose your home as well.

Get Out of Debt

When there really is no other way out, you'll need to file for a Chapter 7 personal bankruptcy. Try looking at it in a positive light, however.

There are some advantages to filing for bankruptcy. By far the most important advantage is that debtors may obtain a fresh financial start. Consumers who are eligible for Chapter 7 may be forgiven (discharged from) most unsecured debts.

A secured debt is one which the creditor is entitled to collect by seizing and selling certain assets of the debtor if payments are missed, such as a home mortgage or car loan. With those two major exceptions, most consumer debts are unsecured. You may be able to keep (that is, exempt) many of your assets, although state laws vary widely in defining which assets you may keep.

Collection efforts must stop as soon as you file for bankruptcy under Chapter 7 or Chapter 13. As soon as your petition is filed, there is by law an automatic stay, which prohibits most collection activity.

If a creditor continues to try to collect the debt, the creditor may be cited for contempt of court or ordered to pay damages. The stay applies even to the loan that you may have obtained to buy your car. If you continue to make payments, it is unlikely that your creditor will do anything.

However, if you miss payments your creditor will probably petition to have the stay lifted in order either to repossess the car or to renegotiate the loan.

You cannot be fired from your job solely because you filed for bankruptcy.

Of course, there are disadvantages to filing for bankruptcy. Since your bankruptcy filing will remain on your credit record for up to ten years, it may affect your future finances. A bankruptcy is a troublesome item in your credit record, but often debtors who file already have a troublesome history.

In one respect, bankruptcy may improve your credit records. Because Chapter 7 provides for a discharge of debts no more than once every eight years, lenders know that a credit applicant who has just emerged from Chapter 7 cannot soon repeat the process.

Research in this area has produced mixed results. A study by the Credit Research Center at Purdue University found that about one-third of consumers who filed for bankruptcy had obtained lines of credit within three years of filing; one-half had obtained them within five years.

However, the new credit itself may reflect the record of bankruptcy. For example, if you might have been eligible for a bank card with a 14 percent rate before bankruptcy, the best card that you can get after bankruptcy might carry a rate of 20 percent—or you might have to rely on a card secured by a deposit that you make with the credit card issuer.

There are a couple of ways you can go about filing for bankruptcy. The most reliable is to secure a bankruptcy attorney and have them do it for you. They are experts in this area and will often take care of everything for you including appearing in court on your behalf.

They do charge a fee for this service, however. That fee can range anywhere from $500 to $2,000 depending on your area. Yes, it is odd that they'll charge that high a fee to file a bankruptcy for someone who doesn't have money in the first place, but many will accept payments.

Get Out of Debt

You can also file the bankruptcy yourself. There are many places on the Internet where you can download the forms you will need. Be advised that they are often lengthy and in-depth, but they are fairly straight-forward when you take the time to fill them out completely.

Once you have the forms all filled out, take them to your local courthouse and pay the filing fee which is usually around $100 to $200. You will receive a notice of a court date at which time you will need to show up and the judge will grant your request for bankruptcy.

The bad part about filing yourself is that you have to contact all your creditors yourself to let them know that the bankruptcy has been filed. You have to be very careful to list each and every one of your debts so they will apply under the discharge order. If you miss even one, you will have to pay it after the bankruptcy is granted.

Filing for bankruptcy might not be your only option. One of the newest trends in achieving financial freedom and a good credit score is to secure the services of a credit counseling or debt consolidation company. But do they work?

CHAPTER 5- TIPS ON HOW TO GET OUT OF DEBT – GET YOUR CREDIT SCORE ON TRACK

Don't despair if you find yourself with a less than desirable credit score and credit history. You are human and can make mistakes. It's natural. The key to this is recognize that your spending habits are out of control, your credit has been damaged, and then vow to never get yourself back in the same situation after you have gotten your credit repaired.

First, get your credit report. Get one from all three agencies. You get one free and then you'll probably have to pay around $10 a piece for the other two. It's important to get reports from all three agencies so that you have a full picture of your credit history.

Get Out of Debt

Some companies only report to one agency. Some report to all three. But if you are committed to repairing your credit, you need all three so that you don't miss anything.

Then go over those credit reports carefully. See the section above on how to read these credit reports. Check to see that there are no errors such as a bill you've paid but that is still being shown as owed.

People at credit bureaus are human too and make mistakes just like you! If you don't call attention to these mistakes, no one else will. We'll cover correcting those mistakes a little bit later.

The next part involves pulling out those accounts that are delinquent and making a re-payment plan. Unless you are declaring bankruptcy, you'll still need to pay your debts and doing so can go a long way towards improving your credit history.

Creditors will see that you are doing the best you can to get back on your feet and this improves your credibility. If all the bills are too overwhelming for you to consider paying back at once, just concentrate on one at a time. Break them into pieces, contact the company and let them know you are trying to come up with a repayment plan and if there's anything they can do to help you out.

These companies really just want their money in the long run, so they are going to be willing to help you. Once that company is paid off, move on to the next one until everyone is paid off.

After that happens, it's not like your credit is immediately pristine. Late payments and charged-off accounts remain on your report for seven years; bankruptcies for 10.

Most creditors, however, look for a pattern of payment rather than focusing on one-time or rare occurrences. That's why consistent on-time bill payments will improve those blemishes.

As soon as you have paid off your creditors, then you can start all over again. Follow the steps given above in the section about establishing credit. Nothing can compare to consistent, on-time bill payments and responsible credit practices when it comes to repairing your credit. Experts say the average time required rebuilding one's credit to the point at which you can be accepted for a major credit card or small loan is approximately two years.

Here are some other things to consider when trying repairing your credit:

• Pay down your credit cards. Paying off your installment loans (mortgage, auto, student, etc.) can help your score, but typically not as dramatically as paying down - or paying off - revolving accounts like credit cards. The credit-scoring formulas like to see a nice, big gap between the amount of credit you're using and your available credit limits. Getting your balances below 30% of the credit limit on each card can really help. While most debt gurus recommend paying off the highest-rate card first, a better strategy here is to pay down the cards that are closest to their limits.

•

• Use your cards lightly. Racking up big balances can hurt your score, regardless of whether you pay your bill in full each month. What's typically reported to the credit bureaus, and thus calculated into your score, is the balance reported on your last statement. That doesn't mean paying off your balances each month isn't financially smart - it is - just that the credit score doesn't care.

You typically can increase your score by limiting your charges to 30% or less of a card's limit. If you're having trouble keeping track, consider using a check register to track your spending, logging into your account frequently at the issuer's Web site, or using personal finance software like Microsoft Money or Quicken, which can download your transactions and balances automatically.

• Check your limits. Your score might be artificially depressed if your lender is showing a lower limit than you've actually got. Most credit-card issuers will quickly update this information if you ask.

If your issuer makes it a policy not to report consumers' limits, however - as is the usual case with American Express cards and those issued by Capital One - the bureaus typically use your highest balance as a proxy for your credit limit.

You may see the problem here: If you consistently charge the same amount each month - say $2,000 to $2,500 - it may look to the credit scoring formula like you're regularly maxing out that card.

You could go on a wild spending spree to raise the limit, but a more sober solution would simply be to pay your balance down or off before your statement period closes.

Check your last statement to see which day of the month that typically is, then go to the issuer's Web site about a week in advance of closing and pay off what you owe. It won't raise your reported limit, but it will widen the gap between that limit and your closing balance, which should boost your score.

• Dust off an old card. The older your credit history, the better. But if you stop using your oldest cards, the issuers may stop updating those accounts at the credit bureaus. The accounts will still appear, but they won't be given as much weight in the credit-scoring formula as your active accounts. That's why many financial companies recommend to their clients that they use their oldest cards every few months to charge a small amount, paying it off in full when the statement arrives.

• Get some goodwill. If you've been a good customer, a lender might agree to simply erase that one late payment from your credit history. You usually have to make the request in writing, and your chances for a "goodwill adjustment" improve the better your record with the company (and the better your credit in general). But it can't hurt to ask.

A longer-term solution for more-troubled accounts is to ask that they be "re-aged." If the account is still open, the lender might erase previous delinquencies if you make a series of 12 or so on-time payments.

When trying to improve your credit score or credit history, avoid any of the following:

• Consolidating your accounts. Applying for a new account can ding your score. So, too, can transferring balances from a high-limit card to a lower limit one, or concentrating all or most of your credit-card balances onto a single card. In general, it's better to have smaller balances on a few cards than a big balance on one.

• Applying for new credit if you've already got plenty. On the other hand, applying for and getting an installment loan can help your score if you don't have any installment accounts, or you're trying to recover from a credit disaster like bankruptcy.

By the way, all these suggestions work best if you have poor or mediocre scores to begin with. Once you've hit the 700 mark, any tweaking you do will tend to have less of a positive impact.

Get Out of Debt

And if your scores are in the "excellent" category, 760 or above, you'll probably be able to eke out only a few extra points despite your best efforts.

There's really no point, anyway, since you're already qualified for the best rates and terms. Here's one area where it's really OK to rest on your laurels and worry about something else.

If you are in serious, serious credit problems, sometimes the only solution is to file for a bankruptcy. This is a last-ditch thing, though, and should only be done if you've dug yourself in so deep that the odds of getting out of debt are little to none.

Chapter 6- The role of Credit Counselors and Debt Consolidators

These companies have started popping up everywhere. In fact, as I am writing this book, there is a commercial on television for yet another credit counseling company. It seems like they are everywhere. It also seems like they can really help you with your debt problems. But can they?

There are some credit counseling agencies and debt consolidators that can actually help get people out of debt. But there are also others who are simply trying to get money (that you don't have) without helping you at all.

There is a difference between these two types of companies. Credit counselors will help you get out of debt and stay out of debt. That means that they will help you realize where you went wrong on the financial road and then help you get out of debt. After that, they will put you on a budget and offer services that can help you stay

Get Out of Debt

out of debt and live a financially stable life. Debt consolidation companies are different, though not entirely. They also will help you get out of debt, but they do so by working with your creditors to help combine all of your debts into one large debt with one monthly payment. That usually entails getting some type of loan on your behalf that will pay of your creditors and you will pay the loan company instead.

Because of the services they provide, many people would rather go with a credit counseling service. That's because they need someone to help them stay away from the mindset that got them into debt in the first place. There are many, many credit counseling companies out there.

What do you need to look for in a reputable credit counseling company? Here are a few suggestions:

• They should be associated with the Better Business Bureau. The service's website should have a BBB logo and a link to their record on the Better Business Bureau website. Click through the link to check that there are no unresolved complaints against them.

• Many people only think about the Better Business Bureau after they've been cheated, but by then there's not much you can do. Working with a credit counseling agency that is a member of the Better Business Bureau means that you can go to them to help mediate any dispute you might have with the service provider.

• Reputable credit counseling services will be accredited by an independent nonprofit, just as many schools are. One such accreditation body is the National Institute for Financial Counseling Education.

• A good credit counseling agency will charge a small, reasonable monthly fee, usually around $30. Some also charge a fee upfront, though this fee should be reasonable (around $50 tops). It may be possible to get a hardship waiver of these fees if you truly do not have the $30-50.

• You will have to fill out an application when you decide to go with a credit counseling agency. The application must clearly say what the fees to be paid are, what the services to be provided are, and in what timeframe all of this will be provided.

• Run far, far away from any organization that proposes to "wipe out" your debt for you, rather than simply helping you to repay the debt. Short of your creditors just deciding to forget about the debt (unlikely), there is no way to erase debt—even bankruptcy leaves a huge mark on your credit report for ten years.

True, your car may not go missing from your driveway if you stop paying unsecured debt (i.e., debt that is not "secured" with collateral, like most credit cards, unlike most auto loans). But you are still legally obligated to pay the debt, and the possibility of being taken to court will loom over you.

You will likely be unable to get even "bad credit" financing if you still have debts in collections—good luck buying a car or house.

Now let's look at how a reputable credit counseling service will work. First, they will negotiate with your creditors to establish a debt management plan (DMP) for you. A DMP may help the debtor repay his or her debt by working out a repayment plan with the creditor. DMPs, set up by credit counselors, usually offer reduced payments, fees and interest rates to the client. Credit counselors refer to the terms dictated by the creditors to determine payments or interest reductions offered to consumers in a debt management plan.

After joining a DMP, the creditors will close the customer's accounts and restrict the accounts to future charges. The most common benefit of a DMP as advertised by most agencies is the consolidation of multiple monthly payments into just one monthly payment which is usually less than the sum of the individual payment previously paid by the customer.

This is because the credit card banks will usually accept a lower monthly payment from a customer in a DMP than if the customer were paying the account on their own. Some DMPs advertise that payments can be cut by 50 % although a reduction of 10 to 20 percent is more common.

The second feature of a DMP is a reduction in interest rates charged by creditors.

A customer with a defaulted credit card account will often be paying an interest rate approaching 30 percent. Upon joining a DMP, credit card banks sometimes lower the annual percentage rates charged to 5 to 10 percent and a few will eliminate the interest altogether.

This reduction in interest allows the counseling agencies to advertise that their customers will be debt free in periods of three to six years rather than the twenty plus years that it would take to pay off a large amount of debt at high interest rates. That's a very attractive advantage – especially for people who are in debt quite a bit.

A third benefit offered by credit counseling agencies is the process of bringing delinquent accounts current. This is often called "reaging" or "curing" an account. This usually occurs after making a series of on-time payments through the DMP as a show of good faith and commitment to completion of the program.

For example, a client with an account that has a monthly payment of $50 but that monthly payment has not been paid in two months might be considered by the creditor to be 60 days past due. After joining the DMP and making three consecutive on-time monthly payments, the creditor could "re-age" the account to reflect a current status.

After that, the monthly payment due on the statements would be the monthly payment negotiated by the DMP and the account would be reported as current to the credit bureaus. Now this process does not eliminate the prior delinquencies from the credit reports.

What is does is merely give a fresh start and opportunity for the client to begin building a positive credit history. Like all negative credit information, only the passage of time will lessen the impact of the negative marks when credit scores are calculated.

So how do credit counseling companies make money? They do charge a fee to you for their services, and it is important for you to get all of that information in writing before you sign on the dotted line. However, this fee is not usually enough to make them a huge profit.

The credit counseling companies make most of their compensation from the creditors to whom the debt payments are distributed. This funding relationship has led many to believe that credit counseling agencies are merely a collections wing of the creditors.

Get Out of Debt

This fee income, known as "Fair Share," consists of contributions from the creditors that originally earned the agency 15% of the amount recovered.

However, in recent years, Fair Share contributions have dwindled steadily, with contributions of 4-10% being the most common.

There is a lot of criticism, in fact, when it comes to credit counseling agencies and their effectiveness as well as legality. The Federal Trade Commission has filed lawsuits against several credit counseling agencies, and they continue to urge caution to consumers when it comes to choosing a credit counseling agency.

The FTC has received over 8,000 complaints from consumers about shady credit counselors. Many of those complaints concern high or hidden fees along with the inability to opt out of so-called "voluntary" contributions. The Better Business Bureau also reports high complaint levels about credit counseling.

Not surprisingly, the IRS has also weighed in on the subject of credit counseling and has denied non-profit, tax-exempt status to around thirty of the nation's 1,000 credit counseling agencies. Those thirty agencies account for more than half of the industry's revenue. Audits of non-profit credit counseling agencies by the IRS are ongoing.

The lobby against credit counselors arises from the belief by the collection industry that the not-for-profit status of the credit counselors gives them an unfair financial and market advantage over them. The IRS apparently agrees.

The tax exempt revocations seem to be centered on whether or not a tax exempt credit counselor actually performed their mandated mission by assisting the community at large as opposed

Amy Reed

to offering their whole attention to their own DMP customers in a "collection practice". However, that has yet to be proven.

Congress has also investigated the credit counseling industry and has issued a report that says while some agencies are ethical, others charge excessive fees and provide poor service to consumers. The report also states that NFCC member guidelines, if applied to the entire industry, would go a long way toward eliminating the abuses they have uncovered in other parts of the industry.

When it comes to debt consolidation companies, you are talking about an entirely different concept. What a debt consolidation company does is negotiate with creditors to get a lower pay-off amount for your debts and then obtain a loan on your behalf to pay off those creditors allowing you to make just one payment instead of multiple ones.

The two types of companies are similar in nature, but with debt consolidation, the only thing they do is negotiate with credit lenders and then get you one payment instead of many. They do charge a fee for their services as well just as the credit counseling companies do.

The thing about debt consolidation companies is that they do what you can do yourself with just a little bit of work. You can call your creditors and negotiate a pay-off balance for your accounts and then obtain your own loan as a debt consolidation loan. Even if you have less than perfect credit, most banks and lending institutions will have debt consolidation loans available to almost everyone.

Really, the bottom line when considering either a debt consolidation company or a credit counselor is to weight the advantages and disadvantages first. Then check out the company you are considering to make sure they are reputable.

These types of companies can really and truly help people who are seriously in debt. But proceed with caution and choose wisely lest you get yourself involved in yet another problem besides your debt!

Now that we've addressed no credit, bad credit, and people who can help with credit problems, let's focus on your credit report and your credit score. Often, there are mistakes that are on your credit report, and correcting them is essential.

CHAPTER 7- HOW TO DISPUTE YOUR CREDIT SCORE - HUMAN ERROR

As we've said before, your credit report is very important to you as well as your credit score. People are human and the information contained in your credit report is entered in by human hands. Sometimes those hands make mistakes.

Maybe you paid off a past due bill and it's still showing on your credit report as delinquent. There are all sorts of things that can be reflected incorrectly on your credit report, so it's important that you take steps to make corrections as soon as you can.

The first thing you need to do is check over your report and dispute any old negative reports you can find. Say that fight with your phone company over an unfair bill a few years ago resulted in a collections account. You can continue protesting that the charge

Get Out of Debt
was unjust, or you can try disputing the account with the credit bureaus as "not mine."

The older and smaller a collection account, the more likely the collection agency won't bother to verify it when the credit bureau investigates your dispute. Some consumers also have had luck disputing old items with a lender that has merged with another company, which can leave lender records a real mess.

If there are significant errors on your credit report, you need to be sure and get them removed right away. However, there are also some mistakes that you can ignore and it won't impact you negatively.

Your credit score is calculated based on the information in your credit report, so certain errors there can really cost you. But not everything that's reported in your file matters to your score.

Here's the stuff that's usually worth the effort of correcting with the bureaus:

• Late payments, charge-offs, collections or other negative items that aren't yours.

• Credit limits reported as lower than they actually are.

• Accounts listed as "settled," "paid derogatory," "paid charge-off" or anything other than "current" or "paid as agreed" if you paid on time and in full.

• Accounts that are still listed as unpaid that was included in a bankruptcy.
• Negative items older than seven years (10 in the case of bankruptcy) that should have automatically fallen off your report.

Page | 58

You actually have to be a bit careful with this last one, because sometimes scores actually go down when bad items fall off your report. It's a quirk in the FICO credit-scoring software, and the potential effect of eliminating old negative items is difficult to predict in advance.

Some of the stuff that you typically shouldn't worry about includes:

- Various misspellings of your name.
- Outdated or incorrect address information.
- An old employer listed as current.
- Most inquiries.

If the misspelled name or incorrect address is because of identity theft or because your file has been mixed with someone else's, that should be obvious when you look at your accounts. You'll see delinquencies or accounts that aren't yours and should report that immediately.

However, if it's just a goof by the credit bureau or one of the companies reporting to it, it's usually not much to sweat about. Two more items you don't need to correct:

- Accounts you closed listed as being open.

- Accounts you closed that don't say "closed by consumer."

Closing accounts can't help your score, and may hurt it. If your goal is boosting your score, leave these alone. Once an account has been closed, though, it doesn't matter to the scoring formulas that did it - you or the lender. If you messed up the account, it will be obvious from the late payments and other derogatory information included in the file.

Get Out of Debt

So say you've found some significant errors on your credit report and you need to correct them. There are certain steps you need to take in order to make sure that the error is corrected and ultimately removed from your report.

1. Make a copy of your credit report and circle every item you believe is incorrect.

2. Write a letter to the reporting agency (the address will be printed on the report). Explain each dispute and request an investigation to resolve the issues. If you have supporting paperwork, send it along, coding pages to match dispute paragraphs. Do not send your originals.

3. Send all materials by certified mail, return receipt requested, so that you can prove the packet was received.

4. Send a similar letter of dispute to the creditor whose reporting statements you disagree with. Refer to a billing statement to find the correct address for disputes, because it's usually different from the payment address.

If your dispute involves personal information, such as your current address, enclose a copy of your driver's license or a utility bill in your name to verify your residence.

The reporting agency will initiate an investigation, contacting your creditors to verify the accuracy of the information. If the creditor cannot verify that the entry is correct, it must be removed. When the investigation is complete, the agency must send you a free copy of your report if changes were made.

If the investigation uncovers an error, you have the right to ask that a corrected version of your credit report be sent to everyone who received the report during the past six months.

It's a good idea to contact your creditor first, then allow a bit of lead time before you submit the dispute to the reporting agency. By the time the dispute is verified, the creditor will hopefully have corrected the error.

You can also make changes online directly with the credit reporting agency.

When you are on their website, they will usually have links that allow you to click a button to dispute incorrect information.

You can initiate an investigation from many online credit reports by following the links provided and checking the disputed items as directed. There sometimes isn't a place for remarks-you'll simply check a multiple-choice reason for each dispute.

If the credit reporting agency says the original information is accurate, it must provide you with a written notice that includes the name, address, and phone number of the person who made the report. If you still disagree, initiate a second investigation.

Unfortunately, in the real world the reporting agencies often try to sidestep that requirement, giving you standard, computer-generated information rather than the facts you need to find the person or department who made the negative report. Keep plugging away until you have the answer you're looking for.

If your attempts to correct an entry are unsuccessful, you can ask the reporting agency to insert a 100-character explanation next to it that explains your side of the story.

Get Out of Debt

Under the Fair Credit Reporting Act, the credit bureau is required to solve the problem in a reasonable amount of time, generally 30 days. If you feel that a credit bureau has not responded promptly and fairly to your situation, contact the attorney general of your state or the Federal Trade Commission in Washington at 202-FTC-HELP.

If you are disputing something on your credit report, you might want to try the following sample letter in your attempts:

Date

Your Name

Your Address

Your City, State, Zip Code

Complaint Department

Name of Company

Address

City, State, Zip Code

Dear Sir or Madam:

I am writing to dispute the following information in my file. The items I dispute also are encircled on the attached copy of the report I received.

This item (identify item(s) disputed by name of source, such as creditors or tax court, and identify type of item, such as credit account, judgment, etc.) is (inaccurate or incomplete) because (describe what is inaccurate or incomplete and why). I am requesting that the item be deleted (or request another specific change) to correct the information.

Enclosed are copies of (use this sentence if applicable and describe any enclosed documentation, such as payment records, court documents) supporting my position. Please investigate this (these) matter(s) and (delete or correct) the disputed item(s) as soon as possible.

Sincerely,

Your name

Enclosures: (List what you are enclosing)

Another great reason for keeping tabs on your credit report as much as possible is the possibility of identity theft. It happens all the time and often the only way you'll know it has happened to you is to check your credit report.

CHAPTER 8- HOW TO DISPUTE YOUR CREDIT SCORE – IDENTITY THEFT

Criminals know the way to steal your identity, and the worst part is that it's not all that difficult. You know all those credit card applications you get in the mail? If you don't shred them, they can use that to steal your identity.

It's not above them to sift through garbage just to obtain a social security number or a driver's license number. Once they have these vital bits of information, it's easy for them to steal your identity.

What they will do is scary. They will apply for credit cards in your name and max them out within days. They will obtain loans in your name and never make a payment. Then the loan company comes after you for the money. It's something that affects millions and millions of people each year and it can be a real mess when it comes to your credit report.

As many as 85 percent of all identity theft victims find out about the crime only when they are denied credit or employment, contacted by the police, or have to deal with collection agencies, credit cards, and bills.

A study on the aftermath of an identity theft by the nonprofit Identity Theft Resource Center found that victims spend 600 hours recovering from the crime because they must contact and work with credit cards, banks, credit bureaus, and law enforcement. The time can add up to as much as $16,000 in lost wages or income. The number of reported cases of identity theft is increasing steadily. There is no one reason for this, but rather this is due to several ways in which our lives have changed in recent years, all of which make it easier for people to obtain our personal information.

In the United States, Social Security numbers are used more commonly as a means of identification. The Internet has made the transmission of personal information easy and, at times, less secure. Online retailers store our credit card information and contact information in databases we assume to be secured.

Marketing databases not only contain personal information, but they aggregate information on our spending habits as well as contact information. But potentially nefarious employees of these companies could have access to that information.

They can then sell it online in chat rooms where criminals meet to swap information.

Even in the days of e-mail and instant messaging, the postal mail can also play a surprising role in identity theft. Checks can be stolen from the outgoing mail.

Credit card companies bombard their customers and potential customers with pre-approved offers that need very little personal information to complete.

Get Out of Debt

Credit card issuers also send what they call "courtesy checks" to customers who can use them to make charges on a card. Many experts consider them an invitation to identity theft.

One of the increasingly common ways that criminals try to obtain personal information is by using what is called a "phishing attack." If you have e-mail, the chances are good someone has tried to get you to bite.

Phishing combines a criminal attempt at obtaining personal information with another plague of the Internet age — spam. Potential victims receive an e-mail from what appears to a bank, an online payment company like PayPal, or a retailer like eBay or Amazon.com. The message is usually sent using HTML email and, when opened, uses company logos and symbols to make it appear to be legitimate.

The e-mail asks the receiver for user names, passwords, account numbers, or some other type of personal information by saying they are updating records or something related to their account requires their attention. The e-mail usually links to a site that also appears to be legitimate using logos and other symbols of a real company, where visitors are asked to supply the information.

The first step to avoid becoming the victim of a phishing attack is to know what companies do business with you by e-mail and familiarizing yourself with the types of information they request and how they request it.

What you will likely learn quickly is that, while online retailers you frequent and financial services firms you use online often send you e-mail to make you aware of new products or services, or even to alert you when your online bill is ready to be viewed, they rarely if ever ask for any information from you.

Banks and financial services firms will never ask you for any personal information via e-mail because e-mail can be notoriously insecure. So any e-mail asking you for personal or account information, such as passwords, Social Security numbers, PINs, credit or check card numbers, or other confidential information should be deemed suspicious.

Often the sender of a phishing e-mail may appear to be legitimate, but e-mail addresses are easily spoofed. Just look at the amount of spam you probably get that appears to be from friends, co-workers, or even yourself.

If a phishing e-mail directs you to a link using an HTML e-mail, the text of the link may appear to be legitimate, but following that link often brings you to a Web site where the URL (in your Web browser's location bar) is often an IP address (basically numbers separated by periods, like 128.0.0) or a site other than the institution you think sent you the e-mail.

Often a sense of urgency is conveyed in the e-mail, such as an alert saying your account will be closed if you don't provide information. Take a moment and don't fall for this.

A close look at the body of the e-mail itself may reveal typos, misspellings, or horrendously poor grammar. One reason for this is that many phishing attacks are launched from overseas, and many are believed to be related to international organized crime.

Despite all the attention phishing has received of late, there remains precious little enforcement of the widespread problem and there are simply too many attacks to handle. It is an easy buck for online criminals.

Get Out of Debt

We already covered many of the ways you can detect a phishing attack, but there are several simple steps you can take to keep your private information safe that bear discussion. Experts say that educating consumers not to follow links in e-mails is a good way to help them avoid phishing attacks. Rather than following a link in an e-mail, open a browser and go to the site of the retailer or bank in question.

When submitting personal information like credit card numbers, you can ensure you are using a secure connection by looking for "https://" in front of the site's location on your browser rather than "http://."

Speaking of your browser, make sure it is up to date with the latest security patches. If you use Microsoft's Internet Explorer, visit WindowsUpdate.com to see if you need any updates.

Here are some simple software tools you can use to help guard against online identity theft:

➤ CoreStreet makes a free product called SpoofStick. It's a browser extension for both the Internet Explorer and FireFox Web browsers that helps users avoid spoofed Web sites. If you do follow a link in a suspicious e-mail, SpoofStick can tell you if the Web site you visit really is the Web site you think you are visiting.

➤ The EarthLink toolbar, which is also free to Internet users, has a feature called ScamBlocker. EarthLink keeps a database of known phishers, and if you visit a page known to be operated by a phisher it will alert you right in your browser.

Unfortunately, correcting your credit report when you have become a victim of identity theft is no easy proposition. But with some patience and a lot of work, you can recover from identity theft and restore your credit report.

Identity theft can result in damage to your credit rating - damage that could take years to fix. Generally, victims of credit and banking fraud are liable for no more than the first $50 of the loss. In many cases, the victim will not be required to pay any part of the loss.

To reduce your risk of identity theft, protect personal information and do not carry your Social Security card with you. Shred items that contain your personal information and account numbers. Keep your mail safe and store your personal information in a safe place. Order your credit report at least once a year to make sure no one is using your identity to open accounts.

If you think your identity has been stolen, take the following steps:

• Contact the three major credit bureaus. Contact the fraud departments of all of the three major credit departments to place a fraud alert on your credit file. The initial fraud alert is for 90 days. You can ask for an extended fraud alert if you file a police report.

• Close accounts. Close the accounts that you know or believe have been tampered with or opened fraudulently.

• File a police report. Get a copy of the report to submit to your creditors and others who require proof of the crime.

• File your complaint with the Federal Trade Commission (FTC). The FTC maintains a database of identity theft cases, which is used by law enforcement agencies for investigations. Filing a complaint also helps us learn more about identity theft and the problems it causes victims.

Get Out of Debt

• Armed with your police report, FTC affidavit, and sample letters, you must contact your creditors to alert them to the situation. In addition to obvious creditors like your credit card issuers, don't forget utility companies, wireless phone provider, and your ISP.

Also remember any private label credit cards to department stores, for example. Don't forget about other personal documents. If your passport was stolen, for example, or if you have reason to believe someone is using a passport in your name, contact the State Department.

When you are trying to correct your credit report due to identity theft, you will have to provide information that proves you are you. That means digging out your birth certificate and making a lot of copies of your driver's license and social security card. You'll also have to try and prove that you didn't make the purchases that the thief or thieves did.

When you have become a victim of identity theft through phishing, this becomes a real problem as these purchases can be made anywhere with a few strokes of the keyboard, so proving that the purchases were made by someone other than you can be a real headache.

Just try to be patient and point out to the company or companies who say you owe them money that you have filed a police report as well as a report with the FTC and that you have been a victim in other places as well.

As we've said, it will take time, but it can be done. Your credit rating and credit score is very important, so taking the time to do will pay off in the long run.

Amy Reed

Realize that in the long run, you'll be able to enjoy good credit again. Even if you are denied credit, you can appeal the decision by pointing out that you have been a victim of identity theft and are trying to correct it.

CHAPTER 9- EFFECTIVE GUIDE ON HOW TO BE DEBT FREE

There is always a way to get out of debts especially if you organize your money and know how to and when to pay.

If you follow the steps below, you can help yourself by 90% to become debt free.

1. KNOW what you owe.

You must know and identify clearly what you owe; the best way is to create a debt list with details for example:

Name/Item	Amount	Interest rate	Monthly Payment
Credit card	$5600	3%	$680
....	...	...	...

And identify which payment has the highest rate thus allocate the highest priority to it.

2. Avoid creating new Debts. When you are already in debt, do NOT create a new debt. Try your best to create savings strategies for the expenses that you do not pay monthly, for example some bills are paid quarterly. Even though, this bill is paid quarterly, keep aside the amount aside each month.

3. Decrease your expenses by developing a clear strategy and try to increase your income.

4- Do not always use your credit card.

5. Always create a list of items you plan to purchase and know the amount you are planning to spend.

6. As soon as you develop a plan with your monthly income and expenses, you can set the good amount for paying your debts. Remember, as we discussed previously, adding an extra amount to your monthly debts payment can decrease the interest payment and save time. When you have money with you, and you really do

not need them as an advice add this amount to your monthly payments.

7. Being debt free is not only, a way to manage your money, but also a negotiation part. Try to find the alternate with a lower rate. Use negotiations, pretend to your current creditor that you've got lower rates with another one; this might help reducing rates to keep you as a customer.

8. Think before you buy! Sometimes you buy for an item and later on identify that you do not really need it at the moment. Think well before planning to buy. Ask yourself "do I really need this item?"

9. As we mentioned in Chapter 1, we have good and bad debts, stay away from bad debt. Stay away from:

- High interest credit cards

- High interest items

- Big mortgage

10. Do not buy a brand new car when you cannot afford to pay it. As an advice get a used one and keep it for many years.

11. Be smart and reasonable.

Those are some steps toward being debt free, but getting out of debt is challenging but for sure it can be done especially with dedication and perseverance.

When you are asked to decrease your expenses, cancel your credit cards, develop a plan, etc... you are changing the way you live, and especially the way you think. Following the steps mentioned above is not a rule to follow, you must change the way you think to be convinced with that.

Saving one dollar every day or any very small amount of money can be useful for a rainy day or to help in your debts.

Always pay off the smallest bills at first, this way you will save some money and add it to the highest bill. This work in most cases when you have for example 5 bills. You pay the small then allocate an extra payment from the saved amount into the higher bill.

Again and again, we repeat the same messages, keep your credit card for emergencies, do not carry the card with you, and have cash in your pocket unless you really and urgently need it. Get out of troubles, and put your credit card at home. Hide it somewhere out of your eyes.

Take this into consideration; the credit card business is very competitive. When you always make your payments on time, call and ask to lower your interests, this is a right for you.

Nowadays, everyone carries a mobile phone or a PDA (Personal digital assistant) or a pocket pc. Carry them with you all the time, and record your purchases whether by writing a note or downloading a free or paid financial management software, it won't cost you more than 30 bucks. If you are only using notes, write down the amount and what it was for. That way you can really see how much you are frittering away each month. This is the best way, to keep records of your financial life in your pocket every time and everywhere.

So it would be better to carry your PDA or small notebook rather than your credit card(s). When you need to buy something take a look at your notes, and see your total debt or purchases and the budget that you can really work with. You do not really need to buy an item or whatever product unless you really cannot live without it. In most cases, you spend money for something with less priority while you can save this money for something with higher priority or to pay existing debts.

Always make a monthly budget for yourself, if possible do it weekly or even daily; being financially organized is the key to success. You must include details in your budget. Add foods, bills, entertainment, transportation, shopping, miscellaneous and other and this way you will see how much you really need to spend and which is higher in priority... If you can make changes to your way of life and save some money, do so. Use that money to pay back debts and in the meantime you should stop adding to your borrowing by surviving only on cash or debit cards

Are you a student? An employee? Bring everything with you to school/university or to work. Have your lunch, snacks and even your drink. It is better than buying from machine. You will save even with small amount but you are SAVING.

For example, you can save between 1 and 3 dollars every day if you avoid using machines, this way you have around 60 dollars each month saved.

Instead of saying that something only costs one dollar, say if I don't buy it that is one dollar that I can put away for a rainy day or put toward debt.

Look at your monthly income based on the net amount. Deduct taxes, health plans, social security etc... and you will have the net income.

If you are in debt, it is a given that you are spending more money than you make. You are in the red. There is no way to play games with yourself about it.

Live within your means. If you can't afford to pay cash, you can't afford to have it. Pay off highest interest debts first.

Usually, when you have less free time, you spend less money on nights out or shopping. When you are in debt, do not go out for shopping or for entertainment until you are managing your financial life the good way. Find something beneficial to do with your rather than going to the mall. This way, you're reducing your debt, and most importantly, not adding more to your debt. If you cannot keep up, you may enter a debt consolidation program. Do not ever work with private forms or lawyers with these issues. There are plenty of non-profit agencies who are glad and ready to help you anytime by negotiating maybe a lower interest rates or by plans on improving you financial situation.

Even though you do not like to have an third party agency help you get out of trouble, remember it is 100% better than bankruptcy and you will have a debt-free date to look forward to.

Take this advice from someone who work in the credit card industry; pay your bill every single month, whether you have a due payment or not. Look at how much you're late and over limit fees are. You could be racking up with monthly fees which are added to your principal balance and are then charged interest on the next month.

If you're a real shopaholic, go to the thrift stores. They are often charity run and often don't take credit cards, so you have to pay cash. Keep you living within your means and you can find great stuff there. Go to the well-heeled neighborhoods early for the best stuff. You can get great items if you keep your eyes open. Would you rather have a big credit card bill you can't pay or a few scuffs on furniture or appliances that has lots of life left?

It's a real high to find the things you need and still stay out of debt.

Be honest with yourself, this way you are on the road to freedom. Ask yourself how this happen to me and why it happen.

You will need to really assess all the debts.

Look at all your statements. Cut up and cancel all the cards and accounts, except the one with the highest remaining credit available.

You should keep one account open for an emergency; we are not saying that you must live without a credit card.

To get rid of the debt stress, you will have to give up many things you consider needs. Believe it you can live without new clothes for awhile, without buying the latest smart phone, the cable TV, the higher bandwidth internet connection, and much more, believe it or not. You have to face the responsibility and the consequences.

Luxury items and things you want will be more valuable to you, when you really can afford them with cash up front, or using credit in a wise way.

If you are an employee, be willing to work overtime, get a part-time home job or something similar, there is plenty of websites that offer home job opportunities. Get a better income will help you to get out of debt. When you are free, take an hour just to think and think, try to have new fresh idea that might help you in improving your income and/or reducing your expenses. Search and search, for example you can buy the same item with 30% less price from a different store.

Do not be fooled with brand name, a xyz mouse for your computer will work the same than a xyz2 mouse. It is a mouse! Why do you need to spend double the price for a brand name!

When you have the same item with different brand names and both of them have a 2 years guarantees. In such situation, do not look for the brand name, look for the cheapest. There are thousands of tricks and ways to save! Always search and save!

If you can buy directly from the factory do it, stores are buying from resellers and resellers from the factory so the fees are double or triple sometimes.

When your debts are high and your monthly income is not enough to cover the payments, there are ways to solve your debt problem. But the road to financial recovery takes a total commitment. You must decide you want to be debt-free. You have to discipline yourself to take the necessary action to pay back your debts. Only you can determine if you are willing to make the necessary sacrifices to achieve this goal.

Finally, it is inadvisable to take out new loans to pay off old ones. So-called consolidation loans are often offered at very high interest rates, quite often all they do is saddle people with new debts they can ill afford.

Here are few tips that should help:

-Bear in mind that you can solve your problems by simply contacting the people you owe money and get their advice.

Get Out of Debt

-Do not ever ignore the problem. This won't solve your debts.

-Do not panic, there is a solution for everything is this life.

-Create a priority list by taking into consideration the higher interest rates.

-Always have a REALISTIC budget.

-Keep all your bills and letters and everything related to your debts. Do not throw them away. You need them.

-As mentioned before, think before you buy!

-When you take a credit or loan, know the TOTAL COST and NOT the monthly payment only. Do not be fooled with the low monthly payment, know the total cost and the exact interest rate.

-Use the advices and calculations of this e-book, when you know how to compare the standard repayment schedule and the debt reduction plan, you are on the road to success.

-Don't be fooled by those companies pretending to help you get rid of your debts for a small amount of money; this amount logically speaking is added to your total debts. You can do the management yourself very easily.

Chapter 10- How to Effectively Raise Your Credit Score

Let's say you want to buy a house but your credit score is somewhere around 675 instead of 720 which will get you the best rate on a home loan. If you want to raise your credit score quickly, there are some steps you can take that can guarantee a great home loan or any other credit line for that matter.

The mantra for getting a great score is pay your bills on time, keep account balances low, and take out new credit only when you need it. People who do that faithfully have very high scores. It usually means you're being conservative and cautious about credit. It's not a toy and it shouldn't be a hobby.

That's good advice, to be sure, but these actions take a long time. What if you're house hunting and you just need a few extra points to bump you over the line to the great rates? As we've said before, the first place to start is with your credit report. Check it over and find out what your credit score is right now.

You will want to concentrate mostly on correcting any errors by taking the steps we've outlined above. Look for errors such as accounts that aren't yours, late payments that were actually paid on time, debts you paid off that are shown as outstanding, or old debts that shouldn't be reported any longer. Negatives are supposed to be deleted after seven years, with the exception of bankruptcies, which can stay for as long as 10 years.

After repairing errors, the fastest route to a better score is paying down balances on credit cards. There's really no silver bullet, but over 60 day's time, it is possible to increase your score 20 points by paying down your credit lines.

Had a few late payments in your past? If you find yourself in some financial difficulties, you can protect your score by making sure your payments don't go 60 days past due. Some lenders don't report 30 days past due, but they all report 60 days past due.

Even if you've paid your bills late in the past, you can improve your credit score by paying every bill on time from now on. Forget about grace periods. If you want to have a really good record with the credit agencies, pay your debt before it's due and keep your balances low.

One thing you shouldn't do if you're just trying to boost your score is close unused accounts. If someone tells you to close unused accounts to improve your score, they're pulling your leg. It won't help you and it can actually hurt you.

Closing unused accounts without paying down your debt changes your utilization ratio, which is the amount of your total debt divided by your total available credit.

You appear closer to maxing out your accounts. That's why your score can drop.

It doesn't mean people shouldn't close them, but don't close them to improve your score.

If you do cut up cards, though, leave the oldest one open. The length of your credit history is another factor in your score. If you close the account of the credit card you got when you were a freshman in college and leave open the ones you just got within the last couple years, it makes you look like a much newer borrower.

Another strategy for bringing up your score is to transfer balances from a card that's close to being maxed out to other cards to even out your usage. You can also just spread out your charges between a few cards. Try to get the usage on all of them at 20 to 30 percent instead of a bunch at zero and one at 80 percent.

You're not spending less; you're just shifting it around to different cards.

Transferring the balance to a card with a lower utilization could help, but it's much better to actually pay down the debt if you have the cash kicking around.

If you're really into finessing the system, check your credit report to see what day of the month your creditors send updates on payments to the credit bureaus.

They're rarely on the same cycle as your payment due date.

That's why you can pay off your card every month and your credit report will show you carrying a balance. Then, make your payments several days before the reporting date.

All of these strategies generally take at least 30 days because lenders don't report payments more than once a month.

If you're in the throes of qualifying for a mortgage and need a score boost in a hurry, you can speed the process along with rapid rescoring. If you've got legitimate negative information on your credit report, such as late payments or accounts in collections, you're out of luck. But the process of rapid rescoring can help increase your score within a few days by correcting errors or paying off account balances.

You can't do this one yourself; you'll need a lender who is a customer of a rapid rescoring service. Generally, the service will run roughly $50 for every account on your credit report that needs to be addressed, but it could save you thousands on your loan. If a consumer can find a lender who is a customer of a rapid rescoring service, new information can be posted within 72 hours.

There's a lot of information that we've presented to you in previous section, so let's do a little recap on the more important points.

Chapter 11- Things to Ponder on How to be Debt Free

The very first thing that you must do in order to raise your credit score is to order your free annual credit report and find out what your credit score is. Once you have obtained copies of your credit reports from all three credit reporting agencies: Experian, Equifax, and TransUnion, you must take the time to go over those reports to check for errors and inconsistencies.

It is imperative that you correct any mistakes or inconsistencies as soon as possible. This is the most pro-active step you can take for yourself to increase your credit score as mistakes can and do happen.

Get Out of Debt

Look for accounts that were previously delinquent but which have since been paid off. Find any accounts that were closed or any accounts that aren't yours.

Then take steps to correct those errors by contacting the credit bureaus and beginning the process in writing to have these errors removed from the report.

This alone can raise your credit score. Checking your credit report often can also indicate if you have become a victim of identity theft which is something that is happening over and over again with frightening frequency. It affects millions of people and can wreak havoc with your credit rating.

Correcting the problem of identity theft is a process that will take quite some time, but it can be done with patience and excellent documentation. You should definitely be contacting the FTC and filing a police report in this situation so that you credibility cannot be called into question.

This should be done only as a last resort and if you are in dire financial straits that cannot be solved if you just don't have the means to pay off your debts. Filing for bankruptcy doesn't have the stigma attached to it that it once did and is nothing to be ashamed of. While it's true that the bankruptcy will remain on your credit report for up to ten years, lenders know that you will not be able to file for bankruptcy again within that time frame, so you may actually be able to obtain credit anyway after a bankruptcy.

Before you resort to a bankruptcy filing, you can first try getting the advice of a credit counselor to help get you back on track when it comes to your money problems. Find a reputable company that provides results and know that you will be paying a small fee for this service, but one that will probably be worth it in the end.

Credit counseling companies not only work with your creditors to secure lower repayment rates, but they provide financial planning advice for you to use in the future so you are not put in the same situation you were in before.

If you do have steady income, you may want to look into a debt consolidation loan. That way you can pay off your creditors and make one monthly payment to one company instead of several monthly payments to several companies.

There are also companies who can help with debt consolidation loans although you can certainly do it on your own. They can, however, secure loans for you with a lower interest rate and shop around to different companies to find you the best debt consolidation loan and help you get out of debt.

If you have bad credit, expect to take about a year or two to get it up to a better credit rating. How do you do this? Let's review:

• Pay your bills on time. This alone will show good faith to your creditors and have a positive effect on your credit rating
• Don't use credit at all if possible. That means cutting up your credit cards and paying cash for the things you need.

• You may want to keep one credit card that you can use for emergencies – but remember that it is for emergencies only. Keep the oldest card you have as that shows you are not newly applying for credit.

• A good idea for not using that one credit card is to freeze it in a block of ice. It won't damage the card and it will require thawing before you can use it. That way, you will have to wait before making a purchase thus eliminating the lure of an impulse purchase.

Get Out of Debt
• Don't apply for new lines of credit at all. The only time you should ever be applying for credit when you are financial straits is if you need to make a big purchase such as a vehicle or home.

• Monitor your credit report faithfully and immediately correct any mistakes that you find.

• If you find that you cannot make a payment on time, call your creditor and explain the circumstances. If you have been a good customer, they may be willing to accept a late payment and waive the late fees. Try not to do this too often as it can reflect poorly on your payment history.

• If you have little to no credit, you can establish credit by obtaining a department store or gas credit card. Then you make a few purchases and pay the balance off immediately.
• Be very careful when making purchases online. Make sure that when you are entering in your credit card number it is done on a web site that starts with https://. The "s" at the end of the http designation shows that it is a secure sight that will keep your information private.

• Beware of "phishing" e-mails that direct you to a separate site where you are asked to provide personal information. This is how many identity thieves obtain your bank account or credit card numbers and they can run up horrendous bills in a few moments of time.

• If you want to obtain a large loan as for a vehicle, you may want to try and get a co-signer who has good credit. Their good name and credit history can help you get the loan and build your credit at the same time.

• Again, we want to iterate the most important thing about maintaining good credit and raising your credit score: MAKE YOUR PAYMENTS ON TIME! And use credit sparingly. There are a lot of great tools available online to help you with credit and making credit decisions. Go to www.myfico.com and check out some of their calculators. Since FICO is the company who assigns you that magic little number that is your credit score, they are a great source of help for the consumer. At this site, you can find out:

• Which loan is better

• How much your mortgage payments will be

• How much money you can afford to borrow

• Whether or not you are better off refinancing a loan

• How much refinancing costs will be

• Whether or not you should consolidate your credit cards

• How long it will take to pay off a credit card balance

• How rate changes will affect your loan balance

• And much, much more!

You can also find many other websites that can help guide you through not only the credit process but how to get and maintain a solid credit score and rating.

Last, but not least, don't forget the three major credit card reporting agencies.

Get Out of Debt

These are the places you should start to obtain your credit report and get on your way toward better credit.

Experian: www.experian.com

TransUnion: www.transunion.com

Equifax: www.equifax.com

ABOUT THE AUTHOR

Amy Reed is a well-known and liked internet marketer today. She explored the marketing industry during her early twenties and created powerful and useful products and services to help other in the direct mail/mail order business.

Amy Reed understands that there is money in the internet. Thus, she wants to share it to others so that they too can be successful as her even such as young age. She has created different books about credit and credit score, marketing, marketing strategies and about how to better deal with your finances.